MAKING Friends AND MAKING Disciples

An in-depth look into ways and means
to effectively reach the lost for Christ
by identifying pressing needs many in the
community experience. In order to assist those
suffering hardships and teach them about Jesus.

GERALD (JERRY) L. GROVES II. D. MIN.

©2019 All Rights reserved. No Part of this book may be reproduced in any form without the permission of the author except quotations in the body of this book.

All Scripture references taken from the NASB 95 update unless otherwise stated.

Cover and layout by www.delaney-designs.com

Published by the Lockman Foundation

ISBN: 978-0-578-57258-1

FOREWORD

Brother Gerald Groves' book on "Making Friends and Making Disciples for Christ" is an authentic guide for those who wish to take seriously the overarching command of Jesus to his disciples to *"Go...and make disciples of all the nations..." (Mt 28:19 NKJV)*.

Gerald has shown in this work that he really believes that this command of Jesus is not just a goal that we may someday attain but that it is actually "doable" right now! He uses one personal illustration after another to demonstrate this fact. Like his Lord, Gerald lifts the second greatest commandment, *"You shall love your neighbor as yourself" (Mt 22:39 NKJV),* right out of the Pages of Inspiration and places it down squarely on the Jericho Road in service to his achievement of discipling souls.

As he goes about quietly doing this second greatest command, you cannot help but believe that he is doing the first one, *" You shall love the LORD your God with all your heart, with all your soul, and with all your mind" (Mt 22:37 NKJV).*

I am very proud of Brother Groves receiving his Doctorate degree. But I am now prouder of the fact that he earned his degree while following Jesus down on the Jericho Road.

May God help us all to do better and to do more as we learn from one who daily practices his Master's Marching Order.

Willie R. Gray, Sr. M.TH.
*A faithful preacher of the gospel for over 50 years
and a former student of Marshall Keeble.*

ACKNOWLEDGMENTS

This book could not have been written without the love and support if my dear wife Dee Dee. I love you and appreciate you deeply. I would also like to thank my mother for her lifelong example of love, faith, and optimism. Mom you're the greatest. Finally, to my daughter Angela, you are my heart, and to My Nephew Thomas (my son in spirit). You are both my pride and joy. Always honor God with your lives and always do your best! To my family, I love you and may God bless you all.

Thank you to my mentor Bro Willie Gray Sr. A lifelong preacher as well as and Elder in the Lord's church. To my editors, Ruby Dudley, Angela Groves, and Glenda Mitchell Consultant, Netporia LLC.

Finally thank you to my God and Lord Jesus Christ, and to family and church family at the Higher Ground church of Christ. It has been our pleasure to serve the Lord with You.

TABLE OF CONTENTS

Introduction 11

Section I

Chapter 1	Jesus as our example	13
Chapter 2	Visiting Uncle Willie	19
Chapter 3	Resilience	29
Chapter 4	Getting prepared	41
Chapter 5	Breaking The Board	51
Chapter 6	Getting Out of the Building	59
Chapter 7	Meeting the Browns	65
Chapter 8	Man plans' God laughs	73
Section I	Conclusion	77

Section II – Teaching Outlines

Chapter 9	Outline for teaching the Gospel	85
Chapter 10	The thief on the Cross	91
Chapter 11	Clues your baptism was not for the forgiveness of sins	97
Chapter 12	Miraculous Gifts	101
Chapter 13	The Church of the Bible	109
Chapter 14	The Kingdom/church of the Bible in prophecy. Listing of first eleven Roman Emperors	111
Chapter 15	The Ruler/King of the Kingdom in prophecy	119

Bibliography 127

INTRODUCTION

Yesterday morning while delivering food supplies to a local nonprofit, I visited a few of the many good works going on in the city of Aurora, Colorado. My hope is to give you a small glimpse through my windshield into local charities.

Aurora is an eastern suburb of Denver and the third largest city in the state with a population of just over three hundred thousand people. My first stop was in front of the building that houses a group that works with children who live in the motels on East Colfax. The nonprofit provides these tender ones with an oasis from the chaos they often see on the cruel streets of their environment and gives them a safe place to do their homework and have healthy snacks after school.

My next stop was a food bank which has been serving the poor in Aurora for over fifty years. It is operated by a committed group of people doing good work in the community.

Next I stopped by a nonprofit that provides shelter and food on blistering cold days and nights to the unhoused. They also help the working poor locate affordable housing and so much more. We have helped them by donating food and hygiene packets.

There are also business owners in the city committed to helping the less fortunate. A local laundry owned and operated by an African immigrant provides a place which allows the homeless to wash their clothes, and for the enterprising, an opportunity to generate some income. This man offers dignity to the needy.

My last stop was at the doors of a nonprofit that grew out of tragedy. It was established after the terrible shooting at the Aurora Cinema. They provide free counseling for the heartbroken and a meeting space for organizations in the city including the church.

I share this with you to encourage you to come from behind your windshields and seek to help those in need. One way to do this is to support those who are already helping others by providing for critical needs. We can come along side those who welcome our help (and so many do) and offer the eternal benefits of Jesus Christ the Lord to the providers of service as well as to those they serve.

CHAPTER ONE

Jesus Christ our Example

Now when John, while imprisoned, heard of the works of Christ, he sent *word* by his disciples ³ and said to Him, "Are You the Expected One, or shall we look for someone else" (Matthew 11:2-3)?

John whose surname was transliterated "Baptist" (Matthew 3:1), which means immerser was the forerunner to Jesus Christ the Lord. The prophet Malachi foretold of John's coming and of his work four hundred years before his birth. **"Behold, I am going to send My messenger, and he will clear the way before Me. And the Lord, whom you seek, will suddenly come to His temple; and the messenger of the covenant, in whom you delight, behold, He is coming," says the** Lord **of hosts** (Malachi 3:1).

As did the prophet Isaiah even earlier at about seven hundred years before his birth (Isaiah 40:3-5a). **A voice is calling, "Clear the way for the** Lord **in the wilderness; Make smooth in the desert a highway for our God. "Let**

every valley be lifted up, And every mountain and hill be made low; And let the rough ground become a plain, And the rugged terrain a broad valley Then the glory of the LORD WILL BE REVEALED**.**"

John had been imprisoned and was eventually killed by Herod the tetrarch, also known as Herod Antipas, because John told him that it was unlawful for him to have his brother Philipp's wife (Matthew 14:3-12).

Prior to his imprisonment, John had spoken of Jesus before he knew of the Lords identity. He spoke of the sign that would identify him. "**I did not recognize Him, but He who sent me to baptize in water said to me, 'He upon whom you see the Spirit descending and remaining upon Him, this is the One who baptizes in the Holy Spirit.' 34 I myself have seen and have testified that this is the Son of God**" (John 1:33-34).

He also spoke with Jesus as the Lord came to the Jordan River in Galilee to be baptized by him in order "to fulfill all righteousness", for the Lord had no sin (Hebrews 4:15). John initially protested to baptizing Jesus as recorded in the gospels. His objection was understandable, and he voiced it with these words. **"I have need to be baptized by You, and do You come to me"** (Matthew 3:14; Mark 1:9)? Jesus answered John's objection, **"Permit *it* at this time; for in this way it is fitting for us to fulfill all righteousness."** Then he *permitted Him (Matthew 3:15). Jesus spoke to John in the imperative mood thus it was a command and not a request.

John spoke concerning Jesus to others as the one whose sandals he was not worthy to unloose and as the one who would baptize with fire and with the Holy Spirit. The baptism of fire being the baptism of condemnation and punishment (Mathew 3:12; 25:41; Revelation 20:14-15). The baptism of the Holy Spirit was received by Jesus' chosen apostles on the first Pentecost following His death, burial, and resurrection and by the household of Cornelius some years later (Acts 2:1-4; Acts 10:44-48). This was the fulfillment of the prophesy of Joel, which was recorded in the ninth century B.C.

> **It will come about after this**
> **That I will pour out My Spirit on all mankind;**
> **And your sons and daughters will prophesy,**
> **Your old men will dream dreams,**
> **Your young men will see visions.**
> [29] **"Even on the male and female servants**
> **I will pour out My Spirit in those days.**
>
> **Joel 2:28-29.**

He further spoke of Jesus when he pointed Him out to some of his disciples who would become Jesus' disciples with these words, "**Behold, the Lamb of God who takes away the sin of the world! (John 1:29,36).** He silenced the protective complaining of his followers who seemed to be offended by the fact that Jesus was baptizing and "all were coming to him" instead of to their teacher John. To them John answered, "**He must increase, but I must decrease**" (John 3:30).

But now John was questioning Jesus. Perhaps the hardships of prison affected John's faith for a faint moment and caused him to question and doubt Jesus as the promised Messiah. Or rerhaps John just needed affirmation of what he already believed. Whatever the case, John sent messengers to Jesus to inquire, "**Are You the Expected One, or shall we look for someone else**" **(Luke 7:19)?** Observe the Lord's answer.

"Go and report to John what you have seen and heard: *the* **BLIND RECEIVE SIGHT,** *the* **lame walk,** *the* **lepers are cleansed, and** *the* **deaf hear,** *the* **dead are raised up,** *the* **POOR HAVE THE GOSPEL PREACHED TO THEM.**[23] **Blessed is he who does not take offense at Me"(Luke 7:22-23).**

Perhaps the imprisoned prophet was unaware of the wonderful signs, wonders, and miracles the Lord was performing. None the less, Jesus' service was witnessed by those who directly benefitted from his compassion, (the blind, lame, leper, deaf, and the dead). And Indirectly, by those who saw and heard of His great works, including John's disciples.

Jesus's answer was profound and serves as an example for us all.

Jesus's Formula For Service

The Lord's formula for service was simple. He saw needs. He had compassion on those in need. He met their needs, and He preached the good news to them. Granted, "God the Word", who was preexistent from everlasting to everlasting, could do in a miraculous way, things we cannot but that must not stop us from doing what we can (John 1:1-4,14; John 20:31).

When Jesus sent His twelve apostles out on the limited commission, to prepare the way for Him, He told them of the perils they would face for His name. At the conclusion of His discourse, Jesus spoke of the little things that mean so much. Please notice carefully what the Lord said to them. **"And whoever in the name of a disciple gives to one of these little ones even a cup of cold water to drink, truly I say to you, he shall not lose his reward"** (Matthew 10:42).

We are often impressed with grandiose projects and MEGA missions but within the aforementioned text, we are reminded of the importance of the little things. While mission trips abroad to far off lands are vital and I support them wholeheartedly, there are mission fields within our own communities which are much more accessible to most of us and often have the same needs as those far away.

Therefore we should seek to be like Jesus. By being kind and compassionate to those around us. In order to build authentic relationships within our communities by meeting pressing needs and preaching the gospel to the spiritually poor.

We don't have to cross the ocean to make a difference for the kingdom. We can make an impact for Jesus where we are by doing the little things like offering the thirsty a cold drink of water in the name of the Lord.

This book is designed to encourage the reader to undertake outreach and evangelism by first, simply being willing to serve others, and second by pointing out some of the ministries we have engaged in within the community over the years.

May God bless you in your service.

Jerry Groves

CHAPTER TWO

Visiting Uncle Willie

I received a call from my aunt, my deceased father's sister, in October of 2012. She requested that I visit her husband, my uncle, at the long term care facility in which he had found himself. The facility is located in Aurora, Colorado about twenty miles north of where I was serving as the evangelist for a church plant in Lone Tree, Colorado. When I went to visit Uncle Willie in November of 2012 he struck me as someone who was somewhat disheartened. Previous to being admitted into the facility, he was an independent man, used to caring for himself and for his family. He had worked at, the now defunct, Lowry Airforce Base in Aurora for over twenty years until it was shut down. He was accustomed to providing for himself and now he couldn't but had to depend on others for help. All this, in spite of being paralyzed from the waist down and confined to a wheelchair since about 1964.

Our initial visits were comprised mostly of general conversation, then progressed to him talking more and me listening. This came as a result of me finally understanding that he needed to be heard, encouraged, and prayed with, and not preached to. Our visits advanced into rote Bible studies. Initially, I used outlines developed by Brother Harold Turner, former minister of the East Alameda church of Christ in Aurora, Colorado. Our studies together progressed very well as Brother Willie began recalling Bible verses which perhaps had not been evoked in his mind for some time. This was evidenced by the fact that as time went by I would begin quoting a verse in our studies and he would finish reciting it. His renewed biblical acumen encouraged Brother Willie's faith and mine as well.

As our weekly visits continued, Willie would often reminisce on how he was converted to Jesus and to the Lord's church. He would speak fondly of an officer from the air force base where he worked who would teach Bible classes. The same officer that taught him the gospel. His conversion story meant a lot to him and he would rehearse it to me regularly.

As God would have it, I met the officer many years later (through a mutual friend, Jon Warnes) and he invited me to preach on a lectureship at the Lemon Grove church of Christ where he serves as the evangelist in San Diego, California. At the time, we had never met in person, nor did we know of our mutual relationship with Brother Willie. Upon meeting this soul winner, I immediately had admiration, brotherly love, and respect for him because of his heart for the gospel and his love for people.

Meeting Brother Underwood

Donald Underwood did not just talk the talk on outreach and evangelism, but he walked the walk. This was immediately made evident to me by the church's willingness to invite some of the area homeless into the building to find shelter on a daily basis. Donald also travels internationally on missions for the Lord, but he has not neglected his own back yard. God bless his soul for his lifelong service to the Lord.

The 2018 Lectureship at the Lemon Grove church of Christ was on evangelism with an emphasis from each speaker on how to reach different people from within our community. Speakers spoke on varying aspects pertaining to strategies on reaching the Muslim community, farm community, the addicted, the Hispanic community, the Mormon community, and the unhoused community. There were certainly modifications that needed to be addressed which pertained specifically to each group, but the overarching principle which echoed from each lecture was the absolute necessity to treat people with respect, kindness, and dignity.

This can be best accomplished by avoiding prejudging individuals by the often distorted perception we sometimes embrace about a certain group of people, but rather treat them as precious souls in need of a savior. If we want to win people for Christ, we must first treat them with common courtesy, then seek to find common ground, thus building relationships based on mutual respect. In an effort to become friends before we attempt to make disciples for Christ. The apostle Paul put it this way **"So then, while we have opportunity, let us do good to all people, and especially to those who are of the household of the faith"** (Galatians 6:10). Indeed, Brother Willie would speak fondly of the time Brother Underwood spent teaching him the gospel of Jesus Christ. I found him to be every bit of the evangelist Willie described him to be.

> "The overarching principle which echoed from each lecture was the absolute necessity to treat people with respect, kindness, and dignity."

The Bible studies continued with Willie for several years and we would invite others to attend, with limited success. Over the course of several years, as I would go visit brother Willie, some of the staff, having seen me on a regular basis and knowing I was a preacher, asked me to visit others who needed someone to talk to and pray with, within the long-term care facility. Over time, lasting relationships were formed with several residents which evolved into group and personal Bible studies. Having built trust with the staff and residents, the church was allowed to provide worship services there each Sunday, which continue to this day. Several members from the Higher Ground church of Christ attend, visit, and serve faithfully in this work. To them I want to say thank you and God bless you for your service in Christ's Kingdom.

The Lord has graciously added many souls to His church through this effort over the years. As God would have it the first fruit from this evangelistic outreach effort was convinced to obey the gospel by brother Willie. Uncle Willie was not ashamed of the gospel and would talk about the Lord and the church of Christ often to residents and staff alike. He would also frequently point me in the direction of precious souls who had expressed an interest in studying God's word.

By God's grace, relationships within the long-term care and rehab facility have continued to grow over the years. We now also provide a short service on Sunday's to the dementia wing where we sing familiar hymns and recite memorable scriptures. Some of the residents are able to recite and sing along with us. What a blessing.

I am also honored to officiate over the Celebration of Life ceremonies organized quarterly for those who have passed from here into eternity. This provides yet another opportunity to aid and to provide God's comfort to the brokenhearted as well as to preach the lifegiving gospel to all in attendance.

The Lord has opened the door for us to have a weekly Friday Bible study and Sunday worship service in which many of the residents and some of the staff attend. All because my aunt encouraged me to visit her husband, my uncle Willie, at the long-term care facility and offer him a drink of water (spend some time with him in Jesus name).

"To win people for Christ, we must first treat them with common courtesy, then seek to find common ground, thus building relationships based on mutual respect."

Bro Willie passed away in 2018. He succumbed to the pangs of death as we all will someday, unless Jesus returns first. The legacy he left behind was one of faithfulness to the Lord and to His church and a deep love and concern for his family. He was a great role model for spreading the seed of the gospel for he was not ashamed (Romans 1:16).

I posted a picture of brother Willie along with a short tribute on my Facebook page to honor his life and service to the Lord, after he had passed. Brother Donald Underwood saw it and recognized him. He said it brought tears to his eyes. Brother Underwood wrote me a message stating he knew Willie and had taught him the gospel. His experience with Brother Willie was similar to mine. He was a man that did not make excuses despite his disabilities, a dedicated soul winner for the Kingdom of Christ who made friends easily, and made friends into disciples of Jesus.

Rest In Heaven Brother Willie.

How You Can Get Involved in Long-Term Care Facilities?

Many residents in these facilities often suffer from loneliness and they are open to visitors. It is a ministry desperate for workers. Since beginning the outreach with the long term care facility in Aurora five years ago we have launched and sustained a work at a second facility and have a request for a third. Jesus rightly said **"The harvest is plentiful, but the workers are few. [38] Therefore beseech the Lord of the harvest to send out workers into His harvest"** (Matthew 9:37-38). With our limited resources and manpower, it is challenging to keep up with the demand which exists in these facilities. The fields are indeed ripe for harvest and the workers who choose this ministry will need to pack plenty of patience when serving an older and often more fragile population.

The benefits of serving in this vineyard are many. You will bless seniors with companionship, care, and the love of God. You, in turn will be blessed with wisdom from the elderly, and a receive living lessons in perseverance and faith from those living into their golden years.

A suggested method to get involved in this needed outreach ministry is to volunteer or visit a family member or church member who is living in a long-term care facility. Read the Bible to them and to others living there. Trust me when I say, there will be many people who will be glad to see you and welcome you even if they don't know you.

You will probably draw more interest by singing songs, hymns, and spiritual songs (Ephesians 5:19; Colossians 3:16). It has been my experience that many more people gather to sing familiar songs of Zion than will for a Bible study, at first. I have also found that once songs are sung and perhaps a prayer said, people are more open to sit for a few moments to study the word of God. So have your Bible but also have a hymnal (song book).

The key person to contact to take your outreach to the next level is the "Activities Director". This person is the one who controls scheduling events for the residents. With consistency, commitment, and love for souls you can become an integral part of the programs at the desired facility and be seen as an asset by this person.

Please be humble when you seek to do this work. We want to knock gently on the door when seeking to enter and not kick it in. We must beware of the condescending attitude that portrays us as riding in on a mighty steed to save these poor lost sinners. But rather, seek to be seen as riding in meekly on a donkey, who points souls to the Lamb of God who takes away the sins of the world (John 1:29).

Jesus said **"Blessed are the gentle, for they shall inherit the earth"** (Matthew 5:5). Meekness is not weakness, but strength grown tender as one of my mentors Bro Willie R Gray Sr. would say. You will need to be tender and gentile with this demographic of precious souls. As you seek to be a friend, and then make friends into disciples of Jesus Christ the Lord.

CHAPTER THREE

Resilience

Aurora, Colorado Movie Theatre shooting

A gruesome headline greeted Aurora residents and the world when we awoke the morning of the massacre. July 20, 2012. It was an ominous day in Aurora as an evil act was leveled against unsuspecting movie goers. A local headline read, "Twelve people were killed and 58 injured in a mass shooting at an Aurora theatre during the early morning hours of Friday, July 20,2012. A lone suspect and former University of Colorado neuroscience student has been arrested. He is being held with no Bond " (Denver Post).

Nationally the incident has been archived as such. "On July 20, 2012, a mass shooting occurred inside a Century 16 movie theater in Aurora, Colorado, during a midnight screening of the film *The Dark Knight Rises*. Dressed in tactical clothing, "suspect" set off tear gas grenades and shot into the audience with multiple firearms" (Wikipedia).

I have purposefully chosen not to use the killers name because I don't want to give him any notoriety for this wicked deed. Sadness, terror, and disbelief gripped a city during this horrific event. Movie goers were targeted indiscriminately. Some coldly murdered, others injured by random gunfire, but all were traumatized by the senseless assault. Hardened first responders did not escape the misery of this infamous event and many suffer symptoms of psychological distress because of what they witnessed to this day.

The murderer was apprehended on scene, convicted of his crime and he will spend the rest of his days in prison without the possibility of parole. He was spared the death penalty the District Attorney argued for but was denied.

What of the families of those killed and the grief they carry and what of the injured and of those who escaped the bullets but not the shock of the sickening ordeal? This tragedy was somewhat reminiscent of the Columbine shooting of April 19, 1999. In which twelve students and a teacher were murdered, and twenty-one others were injured by the killer's while trying to escape. The murderers committed suicide after robbing so many others of family members and friends.

The Aurora Strong Resilience Center opened its doors on July 11, 2013 for the purpose of helping those heal who had suffered from the mass theatre shooting. I attended the grand opening of the Aurora Strong Resilience Center (ASRC) hoping to be of some assistance. I wanted to help though I didn't know what to do, but hoped, just being there, would be a good start.

I made sure to introduce myself to the director of the center at the time whose name was Grace. She seemed pleased to have us there and cordially invited us to help in any way we could.

I began by making myself available to talk with people who frequented the center. Over the last five and a half years our relationship has continued to blossom with the Aurora Strong Resilience Center. So much so, that it has served as our headquarters for campaigns for the students from the Bear Valley Bible Institute when they came to knock doors and otherwise evangelize in Aurora. The Lord has further opened doors as I began having personal studies with some of the visitors. This grew into an ongoing Wednesday morning Bible study which is now a women's class led by sisters from the Higher Ground church of Christ.

To God be the glory for when we don't know what to do or how to go about it, if we but seek to be like Jesus and go about doing good, God will direct our steps (Acts 10:38).

Having the Compassion of Christ

"**Jesus wept**" (John 11:35), is a brief yet weighty verse in the Bible. The setting for the text is as follows. The Lord Jesus delayed coming when He heard of Lazarus' illness. He had a greater sign in mind than healing a sick friend but rather Jesus would glorify God by raising him from the dead. In the midst of the grief-stricken friends and family of the dearly departed, our Lord empathized with them and He wept. When the crowd witnessed the tears of God they responded with "**see how He loved him**" (John 11:36). Jesus would indeed raise Lazarus from the dead but in the meantime, He identified with the sadness of the people. What a wonderful example Christ has left for us as brothers and sisters in Christ.

Let us do likewise by holding one another up through times of trouble and cheering on one another in times of celebration. For in so doing we will be like Jesus. Let's "**Rejoice with those who rejoice and weep with those who weep**" (Romans 12:15). For we are all in this together. The scripture takes us further to those outside the body as well. The inspired text teaches, "**Do not withhold good from those to whom it is due, When it is in the power of your hand to do** *so* (Proverbs 3:27). This certainly includes those outside of the body of Christ as well. Thus we must extend God's compassion to all (Galatians 6:10; Proverbs 3:28).

"It is easier to build strong children than to repair broken men." —Fredrick Douglas

We decided to focus much of our attention on the young through our efforts at the Resilience Center. Fredrick Douglas was a former slave, author, statesman, speaker, and abolitionist. He understood the importance of pointing children in the right direction in order to avoid as many of life's pitfalls as possible. King Solomon spoke words akin to these in the book of Proverbs when he said, **"train a child in the way he should go, Even when he is old he will not depart from it"** (Proverbs 22:6 NASB).

It was with this determination that I began praying to God for direction, in order to formulate effective ways to reach vulnerable youth within the church as well as reach out into the community. With the aim of supporting families, schools, and neighbors we sought to promote responsibility, civility, respect, self-worth, and godliness among our youth. We wanted to help those who have lost hope or have never had hope to find it.

"People need purpose and meaning in order to get out of bed every day. ***They need to know they are cherished by God.*** God demonstrated this by sending His innocent son Jesus to pay the sin debt you and I owed just so we could be with Him at the end of time."

The scripture teaches us how to properly look at "our trials. As a device in which we become wiser, stronger, and more resilient. Young people within our reach need to be taught this principle. Let's listen to Paul.

"And not only this, but we also exult in our tribulations, knowing that tribulation brings about perseverance;[4] and perseverance, proven character; and proven character, hope; [5] and hope does not disappoint, because the love of God has been poured out within our hearts through the Holy Spirit who was given to us" (Romans 5:3-5).

People from all walks of life are killing themselves. Rich and famous people are ending their lives. Young, healthy, strong people are ending it all. Experts point to mental illness as the primary cause, and certainly, it is something we have to look at closely. But could loss of purpose which can breed hopelessness also be a factor? According to the Center For Disease Control and Prevention, suicide is the second leading cause of death for teens between the ages of 15-19 years old. In the land of the free and the home of the brave, people are dying at their own hands. Too many people are ending their lives prematurely, perhaps because they do not see the purpose or meaning of living. They need to know God is the reason we exist. To know Him, love Him, be in awe of Him, and glorify Him. God is the key that opens the door to the meaning of life. When we love God, we will also value ourselves and love others. For we are made in His image.

When we love God, we will value the things He values and will not be easily swept away into the doldrums of a life less lived, a life without Him (Matthew 22:37-39; Genesis 1:26).

There were biblical characters who dealt with depression but knew suicide was not the answer. **Elijah** suffered from depression and asked God to end his life because of the difficulties he was facing (1 Kings 19:4). **Job** suffered greatly and lost every earthly possession he had, and he cursed the day he was born (Job 3). But neither man ended his own life. Both of these men trusted in the Lord and in the depths of their depression held firmly on to His unchanging hand.

People need purpose and meaning in order to get out of bed every day. They need to know they are cherished by God. God demonstrated this by sending His innocent son Jesus to pay the sin debt you and I owed just so we could be with Him at the end of time.

> **But He was pierced through for our transgressions,**
> **He was crushed for our iniquities;**
> **The chastening for our well-being *fell* upon Him,**
> **And by His scourging we are healed.**
> **⁶All of us like sheep have gone astray,**
> **Each of us has turned to his own way;**
> **But the Lord has caused the iniquity of us all**
> **To fall on Him**   (Isaiah 53:5-6)

So many young people struggle with life today as they are faced with the clamor of a fallen world tempting them to follow their hearts desire and promising happiness. However most who follow this hollow advice find themselves empty and confused. King Solomon tried to fulfill his every desire without God's guidance, but came to the correct conclusion, **"to fear God and keep His commandments" for this is the whole "duty" of man** (Ecclesiastes 12:13).

Others don't believe they are worthy of God's love because of past mistakes. They may wrongly think the Lord does not want them. They have sinned too much, too long, and to great depths, they think. "How can a completely holy, righteous, perfect God want such a sinner like me?" This is the dirge (sad song) some may sing who have perhaps had a moment of clarity in which their sins have come full circle and looked them squarely in the eyes. Consider the following text by the apostle Peter.

"The Lord is not slow about His promise, as some count slowness, but is patient toward you, not wishing for any to perish but for all to come to repentance" (2 Peter 3:9). The apostle Paul wrote of himself, **"Christ Jesus came into the world to save sinners; of whom I am chief** (1Timothy 1:15) KJV.

Paul thought he was unworthy of saving because of his past life. He persecuted Christians to death and dragged both men and women off to prison for their faith in the Lord Jesus

Christ (Acts 22:4). But when Paul met Jesus, he changed his ways and the most ardent persecutor of the Lord's church became her greatest champion. Paul could now say **"that by the grace of God I am what I am."** Meaning, being saved, and a preacher and an apostle of the way. An eyewitness of the resurrected Lord (1 Corinthians 15:8-10).

For those who have come to admit that sin is sin and they are guilty of it, like all of us have been, save one, the Lord Jesus Christ (Hebrews 4:15). God can forgive you, no matter what you have done. But you must approach the Holy One humbly. For He wants to save all sinners through the one and only mediator (go-between) Jesus Christ The Lord (1 Timothy 2:5). Will you repent like Paul and have your sins sent far away by the blood of Jesus? We come into contact with His saving blood in the watery grave of baptism (Romans 6:3-5). Where the old sinful person dies and a new you is born again to walk in the newness of life (Romans 6:6; John 3:3-5). Then you can walk with the Lord Jesus all the rest of your days. You can confidently proclaim to Satan the accuser and to self-doubt **"Therefore if any man be in Christ, he is a new creature: old things are passed away; behold, all things are become new"** (2 Corinthians 5:17 KJV)!

"But you don't understand. God can't forgive me, some might say!"

YES, HE CAN!!!

God can forgive anyone who comes to Him in faith and He can wash you clean and make you new because of the sacrifice of His Son Jesus. Will you obey Him and get rid of your sin problem today?

Don't believe the lies of Satan that say you are beyond redemption. The devil lives to lie, murder, and deceive (John 8:44). Listen to God, for the Father is calling you out of the darkness into the kingdom (church) of His beloved son (Colossians 1:13,18).

Can God forgive anyone who comes to Him in faith through Jesus?

Yes, He Can, and Yes He Will.

Come home today.

Let's pray for the lost and the hopeless and point them to Jesus, our anchor of hope (Hebrews 6:19-20). Building close relationships with them is the key according to Bill Flatt, Ed.D, a gospel preacher and a licensed counseling Psychologist. He advises us to…

"establish an empathetic relationship, allow the person to tell his/her story, and remain nonjudgmental and supportive" (Flatt 120).

Young people are often impulsive, and it is during those reckless times they may try to commit suicide. This is when we need to pay close attention and be there for them. Lord help us.

Suicide is the 10th leading cause of death in the U.S.
- The annual age-adjusted suicide rate is 13.42 per 100,000 individuals.
- Men die by suicide 3.53x more often than women.
- On average, there are 123 suicides per day.
- White males accounted for 7 of 10 suicides in 2016.
- Firearms account for 51% of all suicides in 2016.
- The rate of suicide is highest in middle age — white men in particular.

Source https://afsp.org/about-suicide/suicide-statistics/

If you or someone you know is contemplating suicide, please call the National Suicide Prevention Lifeline for help at 1-800-273-8255.

CHAPTER FOUR

Getting Prepared

We began our outreach geared toward youth by hosting a full day Mental Health First Aid workshop targeting those who work with young people on Saturday March 11, 2017 in collaboration with The Denver Department of Public Health and Human Services. We had three area churches of Christ participate along with a member of Denver Public schools. The curriculum presented by the facilitators was designed to equip mentors with the tools to effectively reach into the church and out to the community at large in order to help our youth. It was also geared to assist us in initiating a mentor program for youth who may lack a consistent male role model in the home. So far, we have two men who have officially agreed to be mentors. We will continue to work toward building on this promising beginning and with the Lord's help, I know we can succeed.

We soon learned the demand was great with so many kids in need. We discovered quickly it was impractical for so few mentors to try to be everywhere for everyone. Consequently we initiated an ongoing sustainable and accessible program that was designed to bring the kids together in one place and a two month long summer camp for kids and their families was born. The Resilience Center, upon our request, allowed us to host the event at their facility twice a week at no charge. What a blessing!

The sad fact is the lack of fathers in the home or of concerned and involved men in the community is a great loss, especially to children. Consider the following statistics:

POVERTY

Children in father-absent homes are almost four times more likely to be poor. In 2011, **12 percent** of children in married-couple families were living in poverty, compared to **44 percent** of children in mother-only families. *Source: U.S. Census Bureau, Children's Living Arrangements and Characteristics: March 2011, Table C8. Washington D.C.: 2011.*

Children living in female headed families with no spouse present had a poverty rate of **47.6 percent**, over 4 times the rate in married-couple families.

Source: U.S. Department of Health and Human Services; ASEP Issue Brief: Information on Poverty and Income Statistics. September 12, 2012

DRUG AND ALCOHOL ABUSE

- The U.S. Department of Health and Human Services states, "Fatherless children are at a dramatically greater risk of drug and alcohol abuse."
  - Source: U.S. Department of Health and Human Services. National Center for Health Statistics. Survey on Child Health. Washington, DC, 1993.

- There is significantly more drug use among children who do not live with their mother and father.
  - Source: Hoffmann, John P. "The Community Context of Family Structure and Adolescent Drug Use." Journal of Marriage and Family 64 (May 2002): 314-330.

EDUCATION

- 71% of high school dropouts are fatherless; fatherless children have more trouble academically, scoring poorly on tests of reading, mathematics, and thinking skills; children from **father-absent homes** are more likely to be <u>truant</u> from school, more likely to be <u>excluded</u> from school, more likely to <u>leave</u> school at age 16, and less likely to attain academic and professional qualifications in adulthood.

Source: Edward Kruk, Ph.D., "The Vital Importance of Paternal Presence in Children's Lives." May 23, 2012.
http://www.psychologytoday.com/blog/co-parenting-after-divorce/201205/father-absence-father-deficit-father-hunger

CRIME

- A study using data from the National Longitudinal Study of Adolescent Health explored the relationship between family structure and risk of violent acts in neighborhoods. The results revealed that if <u>the number of fathers is low</u> in a neighborhood, **then there is an increase in acts of teen violence.**

FATHER FACTOR

- Children from homes with fathers present are <u>less likely</u> to be poor, to become involved in drug and alcohol abuse, to drop out of school, and suffer from health and emotional problems. Boys are <u>less likely</u> to become involved in crime, and girls <u>less likely</u> to become pregnant as teens.

The absence of fathers in the home is reaping us undisciplined children, unsafe neighborhoods, and overall poverty, although there are exceptions to the rule. With a scarcity of paternal love, children suffer. It can and often does hamper them physically, intellectually, and/or spiritually. God knows best. Until we submit to His design for the family and the home we will continue to struggle mightily as a culture, community, country, and church. No program can truly take the place of a loving, involved husband and father in the home.

Jesus put it plainly when He taught on the importance of the home.

> **"Have you not read that He who created *them* from the beginning MADE THEM MALE AND FEMALE,[5] and said, 'FOR THIS REASON A MAN SHALL LEAVE HIS FATHER AND MOTHER AND BE JOINED TO HIS WIFE, AND THE TWO SHALL BECOME ONE FLESH'? So they are no longer two, but one flesh. What therefore God has joined together, let no man separate** (Matthew 19:4-6).

<u>What</u>, not who, is what God joined together, within the confines of marriage. The home is designed to function as a safe and nurturing place for women and children to thrive. It is within this context that God purposed for sexual intimacy between a man/husband and a woman/wife to take place. The Almighty is not trying to place a wet blanket on intimacy but rather to give us godly guidelines to manage this precious gift. We would do well to follow His command and avoid the dysfunction evident in the home.

Summer Camp

June 12, 2017 was the first day of summer camp. Tae Kwon Do, Tang Soo Do, and Christian character were the words that headlined our promotional flyer. Attendance was overflowing, mostly from church kids but also, more than a few from the neighborhood surrounding the Resilience center. Classes were free but the students had to agree to a service project, to be completed before the end of camp and to good behavior in order to participate in the program. The Higher Ground church of Christ had several ongoing outreach opportunities that could serve to fulfill the requirement for the service project and most of the students participated in one of them. The majority of the class served at the rescue mission along with church members on the fourth Saturday of every month, as we were in the habit of doing. The kids and adults served the homeless food, sang songs, cleaned, and fellowshipped together with the residents and staff of the rescue mission. We were seeking to meet pressing needs, to make friends, and to make friends into disciples of Jesus Christ.

The holy scriptures tell us to "**Be kind to one another, tender-hearted**"(Ephesians 4:32). Teaching young people to help others will hopefully instill in them a sense of thankfulness to God for their blessings and a sense of service toward their fellow human who is in need.

First Fruit From this Outreach

During our first summer camp we met a grandmother whose granddaughter began as a student with us in camp. Both became our sisters in Christ about a year later as they were baptized into Christ for the remission of their sins (Acts 2:38; Galatian 3:27). Who knows, we may have never met them if we didn't offer this free summer camp.

After School Program

We followed up the summer camp with an after school program which was martial arts based. As was our custom in the summer camp, we began and ended each class with a prayer. I give a short Bible devotion at the end of each class as well. I often focus on the tenants of Tae Kwon Do and give a biblical verse and application for the students. For those who do not know the tenants of Tae Kwon Do they are listed below along with scripture that accompany them.

- ♥ Courtesy - students should be polite to one another and respect others.**" Be kind to one another, tenderhearted, forgiving each other, just as God in Christ also has forgiven you** (Ephesians 4:32).

- ♥ Integrity - being authentic, being well behaved a moral when with others or alone. **Blessed are the pure in heart, for they shall see God** (Matthew 5:8).

- ♥ Perseverance - never giving up no matter what. **For a righteous man/women falls seven times, and rises again** (Proverbs 24:16a)

- ♥ Self-Control - Remaining calm under pressure. **He who is slow to anger is better than the mighty, And he who rules his spirit, than he who captures a city** (Proverbs 16:32).

- ♥ Indomitable Spirit - Maintaining an overcoming attitude. **Therefore, my beloved brethren, be steadfast, immovable, always abounding in the work of the Lord, knowing that your toil is not *in* vain in the Lord** (1 Corinthians 15:58).

We expect our students to work hard and get decent grades in school as well as conduct themselves with dignity and respect at home. Our goal is to build up our students' confidence through the martial arts, while at the same time, encouraging them to channel that self-confidence toward good citizenship, respect for self as well as others, and godliness.

"Why did we choose martial arts for our outreach for youth, you may ask? Martial arts are universal and so are our students. Universal in ethnicities, cultures, ability, and age."

During summer camp we had seventy year old great grandmothers training beside their seven year old grandchildren. There were also able bodied students training with those in wheel chairs. Those with normal cognitive capability training beside those with autism and the housed trained beside the unhoused (homeless). We now have some training from a boys group home, and we are very excited to provide a godly influence in these boys' lives. Everyone is welcome, valued, and cherished in our classes. As long as they don't mind praying and listening to the word of God from the Holy Bible for a moment or two after class.

Through it all, an added benefit for everyone was learning to appreciate one another as humans who are fearfully and wonderfully made by God. We have more in common than we don't, so it just makes sense to treat one another with honor and kindness (Psalm 139:13-14). God's name be praised!

At the end of each class we always line up, file through in a single line, and shake hands with one another. The students thank the instructors and the instructors congratulate the students for a job well done. The students are also encouraged to thank their parent, guardian, or mentor who brought them to class. Thus they learn gratitude.

The growth we have and continue to witness in the students that stick with it is very rewarding. We are humbled and honored to be used by God as a light for Jesus in the dark world. Please pray for this effort and follow us on Facebook at Christian Family Community Martial Arts.

CHAPTER FIVE

Breaking the Board

Tae Kwon Do is the most popular martial art practiced in the world. In its present state, it is a result of thousands of years of evolution of the Korean martial arts. There is certainly a self-defense aspect involved in practicing Tae Kwon Do for it is defined as "the art of kicking and punching".

Historians track its origins back as a way to defend oneself from wild beasts and from one's enemies. Tae Kwon Do is believed to have originated during the Koguryo Dynasty which was founded in 37 B.C.- 66 A.D. This is evidenced by mural paintings found in the tombs of the royals (Tae Kwon Do 9). Taekwondo was called by many names and went through several transitions before the current name was agreed upon.

"Taekwondo is one of the two Asian martial arts included in the Olympics. Taekwondo made its debut as a demonstration Olympic sport at the 1988 Seoul Games, and became an official medal sport at the 2000 Sydney Games," according to https://www.olympic.org/taekwondo.

Let's face it, ninety nine percent of the millions of practitioners around the world will not be competing in the Olympic games. But the benefits of TKD are plentiful, if taught and learned with humility, discipline, and respect. One aspect of training in the martial arts involves students testing for rank, much like the military. They must show they have developed an acceptable level of proficiency in the skills they have been taught in order to progress. They display these skills by preforming forms, which are choreographed movements prescribed by the Tae Kwon Do Federation. They must also show adeptness in sparring (which is much like a boxing match) but with more control and kicking as well as punching. Students must also pass an oral test and finally they must break a board. These rank tests intensify as the student continues to advance in rank.

While all aspects of testing for a higher rank require preparation, concentration, and courage, it is often the breaking of the board (or brick if a black belt) that calls for the most anxiety in students. Tears of fear or doubt and even sleepless nights often precede the day a student has to break their board. It is this fear that the student must learn to overcome.

The apostle Paul wrote to the young evangelist Timothy, who seemed to be shrinking back from his responsibility because of fear and doubt. Paul encouraged Timothy to be brave and reminded him that **"God has not given us a spirit**

of timidity, but of power and love and discipline" (2 Timothy 1:7). Timothy had allowed his fears to get the best of him and he seemed to be frozen in his tracks, neglecting the work the Lord had given him to do. Service the elders in the church of Ephesus had commissioned him to do and the Holy Spirit had empowered him to perform through the laying on of the apostle Paul's hands (1 Timothy 4:14; 2 Timothy 1:6).

Many students face this fear when facing the breaking of the board. Overcoming their fears can serve as a catapult into learning to conquer obstacles in life.

"WE MUST INSPIRE OUR YOUNG PEOPLE TO BE OVERCOMERS"

I recently read the story of a young girl who took her own life because of relentless bullying. She was harassed at school and online until she decided to commit suicide. How tragic! A vibrant young person sought to escape her persecutors by taking her own life. Sadly, she is not alone in this but there are many others. The scriptures teach Christians not to worry but to pray (Philippians 4:4-6). They instruct us in our praying to **"Cast our cares upon God because He cares for us"** (1 Peter 5:7). In our troubles we are to call upon the Lord for He hears our cries.

I believe the scripture teaches that God hears the prayers of little children because they are innocent.

> "**Behold, all souls are Mine; the soul of the father as well as the soul of the son is Mine. The soul who sins will die**" (Ezekiel 18:4).

> "**The person who sins will die. The son will not bear the punishment for the father's iniquity, nor will the father bear the punishment for the son's iniquity; the righteousness of the righteous will be upon himself, and the wickedness of the wicked will be upon himself**" (Ezekiel 18:20).

Isaiah seems to indicate there is an age of accountability.

> "**Therefore the Lord Himself will give you a sign: Behold, a virgin will be with child and bear a son, and she will call His name Immanuel. [15] He will eat curds and honey at the time He knows *enough*** to refuse evil and choose good. [16] **For before the boy will know *enough*** to refuse evil and choose good, the land whose two kings you dread will be forsaken." (Isaiah 7:14-16)

*Jesus held up little children as the heavenly standard when he said…

"Truly I say to you, unless you are converted and become like children, you will not enter the kingdom of heaven. ⁴ Whoever then humbles himself as this child, he is the greatest in the kingdom of heaven. ⁵ And whoever receives one such child in My name receives Me; ⁶ but whoever causes one of these little ones who believe in Me to stumble, it would be better for him to have a heavy millstone hung around his neck, and to be drowned in the depth of the sea" (Matthew 18:3-5).

He also said, **"See that you do not despise one of these little ones, for I say to you that their angels in heaven continually see the face of My Father who is in heaven"** (Matthew 18:10).

Therefore we must teach our children to trust and pray to God for guidance and strength in order to cope in an often cruel and cold world. We must instruct them, that along with prayer, the word of God is a formidable weapon against doubt and fear in the war of the mind. Paul describes God's word as "the sword of the Spirit" (Ephesians 6:17). The psalmist describes it is a "lamp" to guide our way (Psalm 119:105). Jesus said it will "stand forever" (Matthew 24:35.)

The words in the Holy Bible can prevent the naive from traveling the way of the trouble makers and suffering the consequences of foolish behavior (Proverbs 1:10-19). It cautions the young when choosing the crowd to befriend as it is vital to one's well-being. If a young person selects the wrong group they may suffer the consequences but if they choose the right group they may reap the benefits.

> **"Do not be bound together with unbelievers; for what partnership have righteousness and lawlessness, or what fellowship has light with darkness?** [15] **Or what harmony has Christ with Belial, or what has a believer in common with an unbeliever?** [16] **Or what agreement has the temple of God with idols? For we are the temple of the living God; just as God said,**
>
> "I WILL DWELL IN THEM AND WALK AMONG THEM; AND I WILL BE THEIR GOD, AND THEY SHALL BE MY PEOPLE.
>
> [17] **"Therefore,** COME OUT FROM THEIR MIDST AND BE SEPARATE," SAYS THE LORD.
>
> "AND DO NOT TOUCH WHAT IS UNCLEAN"
>
> (2 Corinthians 6:14-17).

Young people need to understand they do not need be intimidated by this world but to face their fears and overcome adversity by praying to God for strength, looking to His word for guidance, and picking their friends and the media outlets they choose to frequent wisely. If they do this, (along with the support of concerned and engaged adults), they can face the challenges of life and avoid many of its pitfalls. They can overcome their fear and break their board.

The Life Application Bible puts it this way.

> *"Our concern for children must match God's treatment of them. Angels watch over children and they have direct access to God. These words ring out sharply in cultures where children are taken lightly, ignored, or aborted. If children have constant access to God, the least we can do is let children approach us easily despite our busy schedules."* (Barton 357). AMEN

Here are some thank you notes from students and parents who participated in summer camp and/or after school program.

Thank you thank you thank you, I am literally so thankful especially because I absolutely love Tae Kwon Do Saleyia (student) 10 years old.

We have been truly blessed by this program and it's teachers. My grandson Jaiden has become more of a leader and an exceptional athlete since he joined Tae Kwon Do. Jerry Groves is an extraordinary human being. A role model as a male figure that has been lacking in so many children's lives. His selflessness and integrity show these children how people are supposed to be whether someone is watching you or not. Teaching them courtesy, endurance, respect all by example. I couldn't of asked for a better program for all of our children.

Sincerely,
Toi A. (Grandmother of a student)

"Thank you for my uniform, I really appreciate your support in this"

From Sequioa (student) 15 years old

---

*The kids really looked forward to learning the Tae Kwon Do movements and making new friends. I was glad they learned self-control.

Glenda M.(Great grandmother of several students)

"Thank you for my uniform and thank you for letting me test (rank testing) I really appreciate it

From Jalil (student) 12 years old.

"Thank you for my testing money and for my uniform. I was so thankful for what you did… (student)

Thank you, for my uniform, Taekwondo.
Navaya (student) 7 years old.

CHAPTER SIX

Getting Out of the Building

I think now is a good time to mention that the Higher Ground church of Christ is a church plant. We began our work in Aurora, Colorado in June of 2013. I was the minister of a church of Christ in Lone Tree Colorado (a somewhat affluent city south of Aurora) for two years prior to coming to work in Aurora. I had been asked to conduct one on one Bible studies and visitations with people who resided in Aurora. Several of these people were baptized into Christ or restored back to the body. This success served as a catalyst to plant a church in Aurora and many in the congregation in Lone tree, who witnessed the results, decided to support me in helping to organize the new work. Together, with the support of the church at Lone tree, as well as interested brethren in Aurora, we began this new work in June 2013.

Because we were/are a new work we had to find a place to meet. We began in a hotel conference room and assembled there for about six months. We soon outgrew their small conference room and began meeting in a middle school, where we currently reside.

I thought it wise to survey the lay of the land in order to evaluate how best to reach out to the community for the name of Christ. To accomplish this, I volunteered in a local high school and called parents of truant students. I was glad to hear the pledge of allegiance recited there, particularly the words "one nation under God". I met teachers who had Bibles in their desks and were not ashamed of their faith. From this experience I learned that Aurora is one of the most diverse cities in the nation with people from all over the world living here.

The school district has its hands full trying to educate children who speak over one hundred different languages. Some of these parents often expect their children to work fulltime to help to support the family at the age of sixteen or so. I also met teachers and administrators who loved these kids and loved the Lord.

I believe this experience provided me a with a balanced perspective, other than the one we hear from some of our pulpits and I have often preached myself. You know the one sided messages warning us to be wary of our schools and the socialization that is going on within their walls. While this is true, to a certain extent, parents must be involved and be apprised of what is being taught to their children and put their foot down if it goes against the faith.

I also met people who seemed to live by biblical principles and would help others with godly advice, if asked. From this experience I also learned to see people as individuals and not through the distorted lenses of the bureaucracy they were under, to avoid painting the entire group with the same broad brush. I trust this helped me to approach others with a softer servants' spirit as opposed to a 'kicking down the door' mentality which would have been met with opposition.

Next, I began attending meetings that addressed homelessness in Aurora. I met with a faith community organization called "Aurora Community of Faith" for two years. This allowed me to learn of the needs in the community at large and of the services already being offered. This helped us to efficiently direct our outreach to the homeless in Aurora and not waste valuable time and effort reinventing the wheel. We were seeking to fulfill pressing needs not already being met by others. I made great contacts with passionate, driven, and capable people who really want to help the homeless get off the streets, into a home, and back to productivity.

Did you know 41% of the homeless population is comprised of families and the fastest growing segment of the homeless population is women with children. (National Alliance to End Homelessness).

> "We will have to face our master Jesus one day and give an account of our dealing with the poor."

There's a bevy of statistics that may or may not move your heart to compassionate service, depending on how you feel about the poor. We would all be wise to consider the following text.

> **"Now there was a rich man, and he habitually dressed in purple and fine linen, joyously living in splendor every day. [20] And a poor man named Lazarus was laid at his gate, covered with sores, [21] and longing to be fed with the crumbs which were falling from the rich man's table; besides, even the dogs were coming and licking his sores. [22] Now the poor man died and was carried away by the angels to Abraham's bosom; and the rich man also died and was buried. [23] In Hades he lifted up his eyes, being in torment, and saw Abraham far away and Lazarus in his bosom" (Luke 16:19-23).**

Usually discussions concerning the afterlife come about when reading the story of the Rich Man and Lazarus, but I believe we miss a very important point. Helping the poor.

There are so many opinions about those who have less than us or nothing at all. I could provide a plethora of data affirming half of the recently homeless are women and children. I could tell you about the affordability, or the lack thereof, of housing in Metro Denver or of how many hard-working people can't afford to pay rent and are living in shelters. Of the loss of the breadwinner of the family to death. Of a debilitating illness or injury that demands twenty-four hour care from a spouse, parent, or loved one. Or of a company shut down or mass layoffs that attribute to much of the unhoused population.

Others, no doubt will counter these statistics and claim the unhoused are shiftless, lazy, addicted or worse. These statements are often based on uninformed or misinformed, hasty, and hardhearted mischaracterizations of much of the unhoused population.

For the sake of argument, let's put these opinions aside for now and return to the text in Luke 16:19-23. What do you do with a person **so weak** he is laid at your gate? (He could not walk there himself). **So hungry,** he starved to death in close proximity to a person who had an abundance of food but would not spare his discarded breadcrumbs? **So poor,** he could not afford medical care, but the dogs served as his physicians licking his wounds? To further the illustration, **so naked,** he froze to death because no one took him in or gave him a warm coat?

I pray we will not allow misconceptions or stubborn pride to blind us but come from behind our windshields and see one another with empathy and really learn about the desperately poor. Then, as we have the ability, and opportunity, prayerfully help those who cannot help themselves. For we will have to face our master Jesus one day and give an account of our dealing with the less fortunate.

Then He (Jesus) will answer them, 'Truly I say to you, to the extent that you did not do it to one of the least of these, you did not do it to Me. These will go away into eternal punishment, but the righteous into eternal life" (Matthew 25:45-26).

CHAPTER SEVEN

Meeting The Browns

Reginald and Sharon Brown came to Colorado in March of 2010. Grand Junction, Colorado, a mountain town near the Utah border, was supposed to be just another pitstop on their road trip to Kansas. Reggie and Sharon had been living in Nevada where Sharon was caring for her mother who had suffered a massive stroke. Sadly, Sharon's mother passed away soon after their arrival. Her passing was followed by the death of two more close family members. Three funerals within ten months proved to be too much for Sharon Brown thus she was diagnosed with depression. Reggie and Sharon were in search of a fresh start and it was to begin in Kansas. At least that was their plan.

Reggie and Sharon Brown found themselves in a Colorado mountain town with sixty-five dollars between them. After staying the night in a motel, that meager amount dwindled to twenty dollars. Sharon diligently called shelters and found one in downtown Denver by the name Catholic Charities where they stayed for a while. Not long after this, Reggie found work as a cook with a non-profit near downtown Denver. But something didn't feel right to Sharon, as the person heading the work was a lady preacher. Sharon knew from her Bible studies this did not agree with scripture.

> **"The women are to keep silent in the churches; for they are not permitted to speak, but are to subject themselves, just as the Law also says. ³⁵ If they desire to learn anything, let them ask their own husbands at home; for it is improper for a woman to speak in church'** (1 Corinthians 14:34).
>
> **A woman must quietly receive instruction with entire submissiveness.¹² But I do not allow a woman to teach or exercise authority over a man, but to remain quiet. ¹³ For it was Adam who was first created,** *and* then Eve **(**1 Timothy 2:11-13).

Sharon, being a truth seeker, prayed that God would help her husband and herself find the truth.

In April of 2010 they were blessed to find housing at The Crossing Transitional housing facility in Denver, Colorado. It was while living there the search for truth came to its culmination. Sharon had gone to a local library and noticed a flyer advertising a gospel meeting in the neighborhood where they lived. Reggie was working as a flagger at the time, (a person who controls the flow of traffic during construction), and they both were going through the classes required by the Crossing facility. On the night of the meeting they heard the truth of the gospel preached and were both baptized into Christ for the remission of their sins that same night (Acts 2:38; Acts 2:41; Galatians 3:26). Praise God!

Brother and Sister Brown were advised by a faithful senior sister to come visit the church of Christ in Lone Tree where I was preaching, and that is how we met. They were hungry for the word (and they still are to this day). We soon began having personal studies in their apartment at The Crossing. After several studies and prayers, Sharon inquired if the church would be willing to volunteer in the cafeteria and feed the homeless at The Crossing. The prospect of serving at the facility, and having the opportunity to meet pressing needs, and winning souls for the kingdom of Christ appealed greatly to me.

Fruit was evident almost immediately as residents were embracing the truth of the gospel, proven by their willingness to repent of their sins and be immersed in water for the forgiveness of sins (Acts 2:36-47). Soon, a women's Bible study was embarked upon and led by several sisters from the Higher Ground congregation. Next, I was able to speak on a regular basis during the men's chapel services held each morning at the facility. I was soon joined by several men from the Higher Ground congregation who also spoke from time to time at the chapel service. James Pfifner, minister of the Parker church of Christ became a regular speaker during chapel service as well and blessed the men with his keen understanding and powerful delivery of God's word.

The exegetical and contextual method in which we taught the scriptures seemed to have a profound effect on the men who were required to attend chapel. Reggie Brown, who along with his wife Sharon had completed the twenty two month program with flying colors had so impressed the staff that they offered Brother Brown a job. Reggie accepted their offer and has rapidly worked his way up to being head of security. His no nonsense manner, groomed in his years of military service, and stance for the truth of the gospel have helped many men seeking sobriety, direction, and accountability find it. It was through his efforts while working within the facility we were afforded the opportunity to preach and teach the word to the men's group.

It has been five years since the Higher Ground church of Christ began serving the men, women, and children at The Crossing transitional housing facility. Some of the men from the church have been able to serve as mentors for the men completing the program. Some of the women from church have served in this capacity for women as well. This outreach has also served as a great service project opportunity for the kids in summer camp as well as offer members from sister congregations' the opportunity to volunteer along with us as we serve, sing praises, pray, and council those looking for a hand up, an understanding ear, and the grace of God in their lives.

Reggie and Sharon Brown had some tough knocks in life, and they ended up becoming homeless. But through their faith in God and commitment to get back on their feet they have not only succeeded in finding permanent housing but serve as vessels in the hand of God to help others overcome homelessness as well as the trappings that often accompany it.

Everyone deserves a second chance and the Browns are making the most of theirs.

To get involved with your local homeless population, contact local shelters, volunteer, and serve.

See statistics on the homeless below.

Seven out of 10 Americans are one paycheck away from being homeless (American foundation of the homeless) http://www.americanaidfoundation.org/homeless%20comfort%20&%20care/Homeless%20Comfort%20&%20Care.html**(a foundation that focuses on homeless veterans)**

HOW MANY CHILDREN AND FAMILIES EXPERIENCE HOMELESSNESS?

On a single night in January <u>2017</u>:

- ♥ An estimated 184,661 people in families — or 57,971 family households — were identified as homeless.

- ♥ Almost 17,000 (16,938) people in families were living on the street, in a car, or in another place not meant for human habitation.

Over the course of <u>2016</u>, roughly half a million people in families stayed at a homeless shelter or transitional housing program — 292,166 were children, and 144,991 were under the age of six.

<small>(SOURCE) HTTPS://ENDHOMELESSNESS.ORG/HOMELESSNESS-IN-AMERICA/WHO-EXPERIENCES-HOMELESSNESS/CHILDREN-AND-FAMILIES/</small>

On a given night in <u>2017</u>, **553,742 people experienced homelessness** in the U.S. Over the course of an entire year, in <u>2016</u>, more than 1.4 million people used an emergency shelter or transitional housing program.

The Department of Housing and Urban Development, Department of Health and Human Services, and the Department of Veterans Affairs consider a person to be homeless if they are **sleeping outside**, in a place not meant for human habitation such as a car or abandoned building, or in an emergency shelter or transitional housing program. Other federal agencies have different definitions for homelessness.

Q: Who experiences homelessness?

A: On a single night in 2017, an estimated:

- 184,661 people in **families, including children**, experienced homelessness.

- 369,081 **single individuals** experienced homelessness.

- 86,962 single individuals with a disabling condition experienced **chronic** homelessness.

- 40,056 **veterans** experienced homelessness.

Source https://www.huduser.gov/publications/pdf/home_tech/tchap-13.pdf

Homeless Statistics

According to NATIONAL COALITION for HOMELESS VETERANS

→ **45% suffer from mental illness**
→ **50% have substance abuse problems**
→ **67% served three or more years**
→ **33% were stationed in a war zone**
→ **25% have used VA Homeless Services**
→ **89% received an honorable discharge**

Source https://www.huduser.gov/publications/pdf/home_tech/tchap-13.

CHAPTER EIGHT

"Man plans and God laughs"

Is something I originally heard the great Julius Erving, (Dr. J a famous basketball player of the now Defunct ABA where he played for the New York Nets and then for the Philadelphia Seventy Sixers in the NBA), say on a sports documentary when speaking of the untimely death of his younger brother. I recently experienced an incident of my own which brought the fact that God is in control keenly to my mind.

It was a Friday morning, May 31st, 2019. I had my day planned out. I would listen to today's devotional reading with my bride (check). I would write my daily devotion and distribute it to the groups who normally receive it (check). So far so good but my day took a drastic change after that.

My left arm began to ache as I was sitting at my computer followed by pains in my chest. I became dizzy and short of breath. (This was not at all in accordance to my plans). I drove myself to the nearest urgent care (that accepted my insurance). The nurse took my vitals, drew blood, and performed two EKG's, three hours apart.

The first EKG looked normal the second apparently gave the heart specialists some concern, because they transported me from urgent care to St. Joseph's hospital for more tests.

What was going through my mind at the time? Lord if this is it for me I'm ready to come home. Please take care of my family. Another thought. But God I've got to much work to do in the kingdom to come home now? The thought that cleared my mind and focused my heart? Lord who do you want me to meet today who do you want to use me for your glory?

So I began looking for the one.

I think it was my ambulance attendant. Her name is Gloria. She is going to school to be a counselor. During our ride we talked about God a lot, the devil a little, and outreach and evangelism opportunities in the Denver Metro Area.

I had a book in my back pocket called" The word of God and the traditions of men". It investigates denominational teaching and compares them to teachings in the Bible.

I wrote my name and phone number on the front inside cover and gave it to her with hopes she would read it and come to the Lord biblically, if she hadn't already.

I think that's why I'm sitting in a hospital bed tonight. Perhaps God wanted me to meet this woman and influence her for Him.

My blood work looks good and my vitals are normal. My heart is pumping blood out to my body normally. Tomorrow's scheduled stress test will gauge how well it is pumping blood into itself.

Your prayers are solicited, and God's will be done. For He is trustworthy, and His plans are best.

How will God use you to influence others for Him? For Him to do so we must be willing to touch people, to interact with them, to be salt of the earth.

CONCLUSION

(Section I)

Serving the less fortunate is a salvation issue that is clearly stated by Jesus.

> **Then they themselves also will answer, 'Lord, when did we see You hungry, or thirsty, or a stranger, or naked, or sick, or in prison, and did not [e]take care of You?'** [45] **Then He will answer them, '<u>Truly I say to you, to the extent that you did not do it to one of the least of these, you did not do it to Me.</u>'** [46] **<u>These will go away into eternal punishment, but the righteous into eternal life</u>"** (Matthew 25:44-46).

If we as the church collectively and Christians individually don't get busy meeting the pressing needs of the less fortunate we risk being cast away at the judgment. The time for talk is past, NOW IS THE TIME to engage people where they are, meet them there with kindness, and bring them to Christ.

> **Jesus spoke the life giving word of God from the mountaintop but then He went down and touched the people in the valley.**

Jesus is our example:
> Seeing the people, He felt compassion for them, because they were distressed and dispirited like sheep without a shepherd. 37 Then He said to His disciples, "**The harvest is plentiful, but the workers are few. 38 Therefore beseech the Lord of the harvest to send out workers into His harvest.**" *Matthew 9:36-38

These are the words spoken by Jesus after he preached the Sermon on the Mount, which is recorded in Mathew chapters 5-7. He then proceeded to help many in need (Matthew 8-9). King Jesus' compassion was manifested as He…

* Healed the leper (touched the untouchable.) Matthew 8:1-4.
* Healed the paralytic and forgave sins Matthew 8:5-13; Matthew 9:1-8.
* Relieved the fever of the bedridden Matthew 8:14-15.
* Cast out the demons from those held captive Matthew 8:16-17, 28-34.
* Cleansed those with blood issues Matthew 9:19-22.
* Gave the blind their sight and the mute his voice Matthew 9:27-33.
* Raised the dead Matthew 9:18, 23-26.
* Ate with publicans and sinners Matthew 9:9-13.

Jesus spoke the life giving word of God from the mountaintop but then He went down and touched the people in the valley. What a great example for the rest of us.

The excuse can be made "We can't do the miraculous works Jesus did". To this I would say , we must do what we can and not worry about the things we can't. For a biblical example, consider a woman named Tabitha who provided for those in need.

Now in Joppa there was a disciple named Tabitha (which translated in Greek is called (Dorcas); this woman was abounding with deeds of kindness and charity which she continually did (Acts 9:36).

Tenderhearted Tabitha abounded with good deeds. She lovingly cared for those who needed her most. She employed her modest God-given talents to make clothing for widows in Joppa, and they loved her for it (Acts 9:39).

How can we make a difference in the lives of others? Differences that will meet a pressing need and glorify God in heaven?

♥ Let's develop a loving lifestyle so good deeds flow from us naturally.

♥ Let's not dismiss kind deeds as casual and simple (greetings visitors, cleaning up after a cookout, working in the nursery) they may mean the world to someone.

♥ Let's be energetic about the little moments in our ordinary days. Offering a drink is a simple gesture of care and concern. Simple gestures can serve as building blocks to a much bigger story.

Tabitha's tender heart and willing hands were woven into the tapestry of the everyday lives of others was profound. More importantly, her life played a pivotal role in bringing many souls to Christ. Let's seek to do the same. Read Acts 9:36-43 for the rest of the story.

How Can You Help?

♥ Can you help a kid with reading, writing, or arithmetic? Volunteer at an after school program or better yet start your own using the Bible as the reading curriculum..

♥ Can you drive a car? You can help seniors get back and forth to appointments and errands.

♥ Can you sew or knit like Tabitha? You can knit hats, mittens, or quilts for needy or repair clothing for them.

♥ Can you sing? You can visit long-term care facilities and sing psalms with them.

- ♥ Can you pray? You can pray with them, read the Bible with them, and talk with them.
- ♥ Do have a listening ear?
- ♥ Can you babysit for someone struggling to make ends meet?
- ♥ Can you serve a bowl of soup or make a sandwich?
- ♥ Can you give a cold glass of water to the thirsty?
- ♥ Can you visit the sick in the hospital or the incarcerated in jail?
- ♥ Can you write? Then you can send cards to the troops or letters to the lonely.

There is certainly something we all can and must do in the service of the Lord.

First, we must have empathy for people who are suffering and seek to meet their pressing needs. This may provide us with an avenue to share the gospel of Jesus Christ with them as we seek to make friends in the community and make our friends into disciples for Christ.

Remember the words of Jesus at the beginning of this book:

> **Go and report to John what you have seen and heard:** *the* BLIND RECEIVE SIGHT, *the* lame walk, *the* lepers are cleansed, and *the* deaf hear, *the* dead are raised up, *the* POOR HAVE THE GOSPEL PREACHED TO THEM.[23] **Blessed is he who does not take offense at Me "** (Luke 7:22-23).

Let's go and do likewise.

SECTION II

Teaching Outlines

Jesus also said his disciples are the light of the world (Matthew 5:16). After sincerely befriending others in the community we must teach them about Jesus and His church. God's word is a lamp and a light that leads to eternal life (Psalm 119:105). In order to assist the soul winner and the sincere searcher in this endeavor I have included several teaching outlines in the remainder of this book. For after we meet the immediate need of the body we must seek to save the lost soul for Christ.

CHAPTER NINE

Outline for teaching someone the Gospel

"For I am not ashamed of the gospel, for it is the power of God for salvation to everyone who believes, to the Jew first and also to the Greek", Romans 1:16

Can you define the gospel?

Yes____ No____

The Gospel is the Death Burial and Resurrection of Jesus

"Now I make known to you, brethren, the gospel which I preached to you, which also you received, in which also you stand, by which also you are saved, if you hold fast the word which I preached to you, unless you believed in vain. For I delivered to you as of first importance what I also received, that Christ died for our sins according to the Scriptures, and that He was buried, and that He was raised on the third day according to the Scriptures", (1 Corinthians 15:1-4).

How do I obey the death burial and resurrection of Jesus Christ?

"Or do you not know that all of us who have been baptized into Christ Jesus have been baptized into His death? Therefore we have been buried with Him through baptism into death, so that as Christ was raised from the dead through the glory of the Father, so we too might walk in newness of life" (Romans 6:3-4).

We obey the death burial and resurrection of Jesus through baptism.

Baptism is not a mere ceremony but requires faith.

Colossians 2:12, "having been buried with Him in baptism, in which you were also raised up with Him through faith in the working of God, who raised Him from the dead".

1 Peter 3:21, "Corresponding to that, baptism now saves you—not the removal of dirt from the flesh, but an appeal to God for a good conscience—through the resurrection of Jesus Christ".

Do we have to have faith when we are baptized?

Yes_____ No_____

What is the purpose of baptism?

Jesus said:

> Mark 16:15-16 ,"Go into all the world and preach the gospel to all creation. He who has believed and has been baptized shall be saved; but he who has disbelieved shall be condemned",

According to Jesus, does belief and baptism save us?

Yes____ No____

Submitting to baptism washes our sins away

> "Now why do you delay? Get up and be baptized, and wash away your sins, calling on His name " (Acts 22:16).

Through baptism we receive remission of sins, we receive the Holy Spirit and we are added to Christ's church.

> "Peter *said* to them, "Repent, and each of you be baptized in the name of Jesus Christ for the forgiveness of your sins; and you will receive the gift of the Holy Spirit, (Acts 2:38) "praising God and having favor with all the people. And the Lord was adding to their number day by day those who were being saved" (Acts 2:47).

What if we refuse to obey the gospel?

" and *to give* relief to you who are afflicted and to us as well when the Lord Jesus will be revealed from heaven with His mighty angels in flaming fire, dealing out retribution to those who do not know God and to those who do not obey the gospel of our Lord Jesus. These will pay the penalty of eternal destruction, away from the presence of the Lord and from the glory of His power" (2 Thessalonians 1:7-9).

Lost____ Saved____

God loves us and wants to save us

"The Lord is not slow about His promise, as some count slowness, but is patient toward you, not wishing for any to perish but for all to come to repentance" (2 Peter 3:9).

The gospel which includes baptism...

- ♥ Was commanded by Jesus (Matthew 28:19; Mark 16:16).

- ♥ Preached by the Apostles (Acts 2:36-38; 1 Corinthians 15:1-4).

- ♥ Obeyed by those who were being saved (Acts 2:38; 8:12, 13, 26-38; 9:17-18; 16:14, 25-34).

- ♥ Is how we call upon the name of the Lord (Acts 22:16).

- ♥ Saves us (Romans 1:16, 1 Peter 3:21).

- ♥ There is one baptism (Ephesians 4:5).

- ♥ The one baptism is a burial that requires much water (Acts 8:38-39; 12:47-48; John 3:23).

- ♥ Adds us to Christ's church where all spiritual blessings dwell (Matthew 16:18; Acts 2:47; Ephesians 1:3).

Have you obeyed the gospel according to the scriptures? Yes ____ No ____.

If not do you want to obey the gospel today?

Yes___ No___

If not why not? I am already saved___.

I need to know more and would like a Bible study____.

I would like to visit the church____ .

CHAPTER TEN

The Thief in the Cross

The Thief on the Cross was not baptized so I don't have to be baptized. A Biblical answer.

Scripture Text: (Luke 23:39-43) **One of the criminals who were hanged** *there* **was hurling abuse at Him, saying, "Are You not the Christ? Save Yourself and us!"** **⁴⁰ But the other answered, and rebuking him said, "Do you not even fear God, since you are under the same sentence of condemnation? ⁴¹ And we indeed** *are suffering* **justly, for we are receiving what we deserve for our deeds; but this man has done nothing wrong." ⁴² And he was saying, "Jesus, remember me when You come in Your kingdom!" ⁴³ And He said to him, "Truly I say to you, today you shall be with Me in Paradise."**

I. How do you know the thief wasn't previously baptized?

    A. He could have been a former disciple of John the baptizer.

    B. He could have been a former disciple of Jesus.

i. He recognized Jesus as a King with a Kingdom.

ii. This would be consistent with **Jesus'** and **John's** preaching-(Matthew 3:1-2; **Jesus'** preaching (Matthew 4: 17). As well as Jesus' **twelve disciples** (Matthew 10:7, and **the seventy** (Luke 10:9).

C. John the Baptist and Jesus would baptize the people they taught (Mark 1:4; John 3:3-5; John 3:22, 23; John 4:1-2).

D. John's baptism" was for the remission of sins" (Mark 1:4; John 3:1-5; John 4:1-2).

Jesus answered, "Truly, truly, I say to you, unless one is born of water and the Spirit he cannot enter into the kingdom of God (John 3:5).

E. Those who refused John's baptism were seen as those who "rejected the counsel of God" (Luke 7:30).

I say to you, among those born of women there is no one greater than John; yet he who is least in the kingdom of God is greater than he." [29] When all the people and the tax collectors heard this, <u>they acknowledged God's justice, having been baptized</u> with the baptism of John. [30] But the Pharisees and the <u>lawyers rejected God's purpose for themselves, not having been baptized</u> by John

II. Jesus had the authority to forgive sins while he was on earth (Matthew 9:1-6; Mark 2:5-10; Luke 5:20-24).

Which is easier, to say, 'Your sins are forgiven,' or to say, 'Get up, and walk'? ⁶ But so that you may know that the Son of Man has authority on earth to forgive sins (Matthew 9:6a)

    A. Jesus is Divine (John 1:1-4, 14, 18; Hebrews 1:1-3, 8-13).

    B. God the Father has given Judgement over to the Son (John 5:21-23).

    C. Jesus forgave the sins of people while on earth.

    D. As the "only judge and lawgiver" Jesus has the authority to forgive sins or pronounce judgement (James 4:12).

III. After Jesus died and rose from the dead He commanded His followers to preach the gospel.

    A. **And He said to them, "Go into all the world and preach the gospel to all creation. ¹⁶ He who has believed and has been baptized shall be saved; but he who has disbelieved shall be condemned** (Mark 16:16).

B. **Go therefore and make disciples of all the nations, baptizing them in the name of the Father and the Son and the Holy Spirit** (Matthew 28:19).

C. On the day the church began, and people asked to be saved Peter said: **"Repent, and each of you be baptized in the name of Jesus Christ for the forgiveness of your sins; and you will receive the gift of the Holy Spirit**(Acts 2:38).

D. **Those who wished to be saved obeyed the same day and hour, So then, those who had received his word were baptized; and that day there were added about three thousand souls** (Acts 2:41).

E. The saving gospel is the death, burial and resurrection of Jesus Christ (1 Corinthians 15:1-4). Jesus could not command the thief to obey something that had not taken place yet, for at the time Jesus had not died and risen (Romans 6:3-4; Colossians 2:11-12).

Conclusion: There is no way of knowing if the thief was previously baptized or not. To say he wasn't is to make an assumption not backed up by any evidence. Jesus' and John's preaching was to **"repent for the kingdom of heaven is at hand"**. John the Baptist and Jesus baptized the people they taught. To say you don't need to be baptized (immersed) to be saved is teaching contrary to the clear command of Jesus.

The apostles also baptized the people they taught and re-baptized people who did not have a clear understanding (Acts 2:38; 19:1-6).

Jesus commands baptism for those who believe in Him and want to be saved (Mark 16:16). Why argue with the Lord? Don't be numbered with the Pharisees who rejected the will God had for them by refusing to be baptized by John's baptism. But rather be like the 3000 men on the day of Pentecost who asked Peter and the rest of the Apostles, "what must we do to be saved". **Then repent and be baptized in the name of Jesus for the remission of your sins** (Acts 2:38).

Do it today.

CHAPTER ELEVEN

Clues your baptism was not for the forgiveness of sins

I. It was not an immersion

And he ordered the chariot to stop; and they both went down into the water, Philip as well as the eunuch, and he baptized him. ³⁹ When they came up out of the water, the Spirit of the Lord snatched Philip away; and the eunuch no longer saw him, but went on his way rejoicing (Acts 8:38-39).

    A. *Baptizo*- immerse- to dip, submerge- (Acts 8:38-39; Romans 6:3-4).

    B. *Rhantizo*- sprinkled –(Hebrews 9:19,21; 10:22).

    C. *Katacheo*-poured (Matthew 26:7) *Balo* – poured- (Matthew 26:12).

II. There was no proper teaching involved on what baptism is, what it's for and what it does (John 6:45).

A. It requires faith in the working of God (Colossians 2:11-12; Romans 14:23; Hebrews 11:6).

B. It's for the forgiveness of sins (Acts 2:38; 22:16).

C. It's where we reach the cleansing blood of Jesus (John 19: 33, 34; Romans 6:3-4; Ephesians 1:7; Hebrews 9:22).

D. It's a washing away of our sins (Acts 22:16; Titus 3:5,6).

E. It's when we are added to Christ's church (Acts 2:47; Gal 3:26-28; Romans 16:16).

F. It's when we become children of God (Galatians 3:26-27).

III. You had to wait for "baptism Sunday" or another special occasion to be baptized.

A. People in the Bible were baptized the same day (Acts 2:41).

B. People in the Bible were baptized the same night (Acts 16:30-33).

C. People in the Bible were baptized the same hour (Acts 8:38; 10:47-48; 22:16)

IV. The person did not understand what was going on, "baptized as a baby"

A. Babies are innocent and do not inherit the sins of the fathers (Deuteronomy 24:16; Ezekiel 18:1-4, 20; Jeremiah 31:29; [Exodus32:31-33; Romans 9:1-3] 2 Corinthians 5:10).

B. Babies cannot repent and have nothing to repent of (Acts 2:38).

C. Babies cannot confess Jesus (Matthew 10:32,33; Romans 10:9.10).

D. Babies cannot exercise free will to accept or reject the gospel message (Acts 2:36, Romans 10:12-14).

E. A baby has not reached the age of accountability and does not understand the difference between right and wrong thus is innocent (Isaiah 7:14-16; Matthew 18:1-4; Matthew 19:13-14).

Conclusion: Biblical baptism is an immersion in water for the forgiveness of sins. It is administered to those who are taught, can understand, and by their own free will, believe, repent, confess, and are baptized. Baptism is administered right away as it is the point at which we are saved by coming into contact with the blood of Jesus. Thus God forgives us for our sins, adopts us as His children, and adds us to Jesus' church. Baptism is not "an outward sign of an inward grace" but an answer of a good conscience to God (1Peter 3:20, 21).

If you are interested please contact the Higher Ground church of Christ at info@hgcoc.org.

CHAPTER TWELVE

Miraculous Gifts

I. The purpose of miraculous spiritual gifts (tongues, prophecy, healing, etc.) were given is as follows.

   A. To confirm the word

*Therefore many other signs Jesus also performed in the presence of the disciples, which are not written in this book; 31 but these have been written so that you may believe that Jesus is the Christ, the Son of God; and that believing you may have life in His name (John 20:30-31) NASB

*So then, when the Lord Jesus had spoken to them, He was received up into heaven and sat down at the right hand of God. 20 And they went out and preached everywhere, while the Lord worked with them, and confirmed the word by the signs that followed (Mark 16:19-20) NASB.

*For this reason we must pay much closer attention to what we have heard, so that we do not drift away from it. 2 For if the word spoken through angels proved unalterable, and every transgression and disobedience received a just penalty 3 how will we escape if we neglect so great a salvation? After it was at the first spoken through the Lord, it was confirmed to us by those who heard, 4 God also testifying with them, both by signs and wonders and by various [e]miracles and by gifts of the Holy Spirit according to His own will (Hebrews 2:1-4) NASB.

B. The word has been confirmed so there is no longer a need for miraculous spiritual gifts.

   *All scripture is given by inspiration of God, and is profitable for doctrine, for reproof, for correction, for instruction in righteousness 17 That the man of God may be perfect, thoroughly furnished unto all good works (2 Timothy 3:16-17) KJV.

   *Beloved, when I gave all diligence to write unto you of the common salvation, it was needful for me to write unto you, and exhort you that ye should earnestly contend for the faith which was once delivered unto the saints (Jude 3) KJV.

II. How were miraculous spiritual gifts administered?

A. Baptism of the Holy Spirit promised in the 9th Century B.C. In the book of Joel 2:28, and Matthew 3:11. John the baptizer said I baptize you with water but there is one coming after me whose shoes I am unworthy to untie. He shall baptize you with the Holy Spirit and with Fire. Acts 1:4-5. Fire is not the H.S. baptism but hell (Matthew 25:41; Revelation 20:14-15).

   1. All flesh (all mankind). The Apostles represented the Jews (Acts 1:4-5).
   2. The Gentiles were represented by the household of Cornelius (Acts 10-11).

      a) The Apostles were baptized in the H.S. to remember all things Jesus had said to them (John 14:26. So that the Holy Spirt to guide them in all truth (John 16:13).

      b) Cornelius and his household were baptized in the Holy Spirit to show the Jews that the Gentiles could become Christians thus accepted by God into one family (Acts 10:44-47; Acts 11:15-18).

B. Paul wrote the letter of Ephesians in A.D. 62. Ephesians 4:5 records there is one baptism. Which one was it?

1. The baptism in water for the remission of sins is the one that is it last "**until the end of the age'** (Matthew 28:20).

    a) The baptism of faith in water is a command to be obeyed (Matthew 28:19-20; Mark 16:16; Acts 2:38).

2. The Holy Spirit baptism had been fulfilled in the apostles (Jews) and the household of Cornelius (Gentiles) which constitutes (all flesh or all mankind).

    a) The Holy Spirit baptism was a promise to be received not a command to be obeyed (Joel 2:28; Matthew 3:11; Acts 1:4-5).

    b) The baptism of the Holy Spirit was administered by God not man.

    c) The Baptism of the Holy Spirit was fulfilled in the Apostles and the household of Cornelius.

III. Since the baptism of the Holy Spirit ceased with the apostles and the household of Cornelius there is no one who is baptized by the Holy Spirit today and thus no one receives miraculous gifts that way.

IV. The only other way in scripture to receive miraculous spiritual gifts was through the laying on of the apostle's hands (Acts 8:18; Acts 6:6; 8:18; 19:6; 2 Timothy 1:16; (Romans 1:11 (implied).

    A. Paul's interaction with the 12 disciples of John in Ephesus proved the baptism of John had ceased Acts 19:1-6.

        1. John's baptism was an immersion John 3:23 (much water and his name means immerser). It was for remission of sins (Matthew 3:5-6; Mark 1:4-5: Luke 3:3). The people and tax collectors were baptized by Johns baptism for this reason (Luke 7:29). The Pharisees and lawyers rejected Gods purpose by not being baptized by John (Luke 7:30).

I say to you, among those born of women there is no one greater than John; yet he who is least in the kingdom of God is greater than he." [29] When all the people and the tax collectors heard this, they acknowledged God's justice, having been baptized with the baptism of John. [30] But the Pharisees and the lawyers rejected God's purpose for themselves, not having been baptized by John (Luke 7:28-30).

  b) Jesus was the lone exception as He was baptized by John "to fulfill all righteousness." He had no sin (Matthew 3:15; Hebrews 4:15).
 2. Gifts given listed in 1 Corinthians 12:8-12 (miraculous)

B. This was temporary. Those whom had the apostle's hands laid on them could not pass on the gifts (Acts 8:1-18). Philip the evangelist had the miraculous gifts but could not pass them on (Acts 6:1-6).

C. Those powers were given by God to confirm the word (Mark 16:20).

D. When the last apostle died the ability to pass on the gifts died with him.

V. Some argue that 1 Timothy 4:14 allows other to pass on spiritual gifts.

 A. 2 Timothy 1:6- Timothy's gift came "through" the laying on of Paul's hands. The (Greek word is dia) which expresses the means by which the miraculous spiritual gifts were given is used.

 B. Acts 8:18 uses the word "through" (dia) to explain that through the laying on of the apostles hands the Holy Spirit was given to empower one to perform miraculous wonders.

C. 1 Timothy 4:14 Timothy's gift came along "with" (the Greek word is 'meta') the elder's hands. The elders did not bestow gifts on Timothy but rather put him into the ministry with the laying of their hands. They supported him they did not empower him with spiritual gifts because they were not apostles and because the Greek word (meta) does not say that they did.

The source by which one receives miraculous gifts have discontinued when the last apostle died. Therefore there is no avenue to receive them. Miraculous gifts were meant to confirm the word and were designed to operate until the Bible could be written down. This happened by 100 A.D. The One baptism is the one in water for the remission of sins that will last until the end of the age (Ephesians 4:5; Matthew 28:20).

The ability to pass on miraculous spiritual gifts discontinued with John the beloved apostle the son of Zebedee (Matthew 10:2; Acts 1:13). The author of 1,2, and 3 John, the gospel of John ,and Revelation. Therefore the perfect which was to come in 1 Corinthians 13:10 is the completed revelation of the New Testament. We learn God's will by reading the Holy Bible.

CHAPTER THIRTEEN

The Church of the Bible

In Ephesians 4:5 Paul talked about the one baptism which we have establish is faithful immersion in water for the remission of sins (Matthew 28:18-20; Acts 2:38; Acts 22:16; Romans 6:3-4; Colossians 2:12; 1 Peter 3:21). Paul also taught that there is one body (Ephesians 4:4). The body is the church (Colossians 1:18; Ephesians 1: 22-23).

> "And He put all things in subjection under His feet, and gave Him as head over all things to the church,²³ which is His body, the fullness of Him who fills all in all."

When Peter preached the saving gospel for the first time on the day of Pentecost he instructed those that asked him "what shall we do" to be saved, to **"Repent, and each of you be baptized in the name of Jesus Christ for the**

forgiveness of your sins; and you will receive the gift of the Holy Spirit" (Acts 2:36-38).

Those who obeyed the gospel of Jesus Christ were immersed in water the same day (Acts 2:41). Others, when they heard the gospel were immersed the same hour of the night (Acts 16:33), still others, as they went along the way (Acts 8:36-38). Once the gospel was obeyed biblically, the obedient people were added to the church by the Lord (Acts 2:47). They did not "join the church of their choice" because there was only one body (church). They were not voted in by a human counsel, but the Lord Himself added them to that one body.

Oh that denominational churches would abandon their creed books and human traditions, forsake their catechisms and pick up the Bible and the Bible alone and do what it says. Only then will we have the unity of the faith that the Bible speaks of in Ephesians 4:1-3.

Have you grown tired of different people telling you various ways in which to be saved? Turn off their voices and open the Bible. Read the book of Acts and do what it says and become a member of the one body now.

CHAPTER FOURTEEN

The Kingdom/Church in Prophecy

There is a common concept that when Jesus came to earth the first time, it was to establish an earthly kingdom. This kingdom was rejected by the Jews. Therefore He postponed it and established the church instead. Proponents of this philosophy believe Jesus will set up His earthly kingdom when he returns to earth a second time.

> "**This concept relegates the church to a role of a stop gap measure, a kind of afterthought conceived by Christ to provide something to fill the gap between his return to the Father and His return to earth**," (Durley 7).

What does the Bible say about the coming kingdom of Christ? In this lesson we hope to answer the questions of when the *kingdom was to come, where it would begin and what it will be*? * Daniel 2:44-45

"In the days of those kings the God of heaven will set up a kingdom which will never be destroyed, and *that* kingdom will not be left for another people; it will crush and put an end to all these kingdoms, but it will itself endure forever. [45] Inasmuch as you saw that a stone was cut out of the mountain without hands and that it crushed the iron, the bronze, the clay, the silver and the gold, the great God has made known to the king what will take place in the future; so the dream is true and its interpretation is trustworthy."

1. When – Concerning Nebuchadnezzar's dream "Times of those kings. Daniel 2:44 (4th Kingdom)

   A. Head of Gold- 1st Kingdom Babylon
   B. Chest/Arms silver- 2nd Medo-Persia
   C. Belly/Thighs bronze- 3rd Greece
   D. Legs and feet iron and clay- 4th Roman

2. Concerning Daniels vision. Daniel 7- Happened during the 1st year of Belshazzar's reign

   A. The beasts = kings *"These great beasts, which are four in number, are four kings who will arise from the earth (*Daniel 7:17).
      1. Lion with wings like an eagle.
      2. King of beasts and birds-goes well with gold- Babylon.
      3. Jeremiah compared Nebuchadnezzar to a lion (Jeremiah 4:7, 49:19).

B. Bear that rises from the sea Medo-Persian empire.

    4. Darius the Mede would depose Belshazzar the Babylonian (Daniel 5:24-30).

    5. Three ribs would be reminiscent of conquest. One idea is three kingdoms fell.

        a) 546 BC: Lydia fell to Cyrus who ruled from about (558-529 BC)

        b) 539 BC; Babylon annexed by Cyrus.

        c) 524 BC Egypt falls to Cambyses who ruled from about (529-523).

C. Leopard with 4 wings and 4 Heads.

    6. Alexander the Great conquered the great near east with great speed and precision.

    7. Four represents the division of Alexander's kingdom by his generals after his early death.

        a) Cassander ruled Greece and Macedonia.

        b) Lysimachus over Thrace and a large portion of Asia Minor.

        c) Seleucus over Syria and much of the middle east.

        d) Ptolemy over Egypt.

D. The fourth beast- iron teeth, ten horns-different from the others.

    8. Ten horns = Ten kings 7:24

    9. One horn after them will subdue 3 kings and persecute the saints (Daniel 7:24,25).

    10. 11 kings in total

    11. Eleven Emperors of the Roman empire. (See insert of Roman Emperors).

E. Medo-Persian and Greek Kingdom named in Daniel 8.

    12. Ram with two horns. The ram which you saw with the two horns represents the kings of Media and Persia (Daniel 8:20).

    13. The Shaggy Goat with one Horn. *"The shaggy goat represents the kingdom of Greece, and the large horn that is between his eyes is the first king (*Daniel 8:21).

    14. Roman Empire would spring From it. "The broken *horn* and the four *horns that* arose in its place *represent* four kingdoms *which* will arise from *his* nation, although not with his power" (Daniel 8:22).

III. The Divine Kingdom: Daniel 2:44-45
A. Time of the Roman empire.
B. Not a human kingdom. (Not made with hands).
C. Mighty Nation- crush iron and all others.
D. It will consume all other Kingdoms.

IV. When and where
A. Isaiah 2:2-3 In the last days beginning from Jerusalem.
B. Micah 4:1-2

IV. 1st century Prophecies of the Kingdom. "The Kingdom of Heaven is at hand".
A. Message of John the baptizer (John 3:1,2).
B. Jesus (Matthew 4:17).
C. The Apostles (Matthew 10:7).
D. The seventy (Luke 10:9).

V. Jesus predicted it would come soon.
A. Some who lived during His ministry would still be alive (Matthew 16:28, Mark 9:1, Luke 9:27).
B. Jesus Promises to build it (Matt 16:18,19) (future).
C. He accomplished His task on the day of Pentecost (Acts 2:47).
D. The Kingdom is here now and is His church (Colossians 1:13) (present).

VI. The Kingdoms in Daniel
- a. Babylon (612-539 BC)
    - i. Head of gold -Daniel 2
    - ii. Lion -Daniel 7
- b. Medo- Persia (539-336 BC)
    - i. Shoulders and arms silver =Daniel 2
    - ii. Bear -Daniel 7:4
    - iii. Ram -Daniel 8:20
- c. Greece (336-146 BC)
    - i. Stomach and thighs of brass 2
    - ii. Leopard- Daniel 7:5
    - iii. Shaggy goat- Daniel 8:21
- d. Rome (146BC- 476 AD)
    - i. Legs/feet of iron and clay -Daniel 2
    - ii. Terrifying beast -Daniel 7:6

"These great beasts, which are four *in number,* are four kings *who* will arise from the earth", Daniel 7:17.

Christ's eternal church/Kingdom was established during the Roman empire in the 1st centruy.

VII. The Kings of Rome (Daniel 7:7-8,7:15-25)
1. Augustus - 27 B.C. – A.D. 14 (Caesar of the Census (Luke 2:1).
2. Tiberius - A.D. 14-37 (Caesar who ruled when Pontius Pilate was governor of Judea (Luke 3:1). Christ's Church established.
3. Caligula -A.D. 37-41
4. Claudius -A.D. 41-54 (Caesar who banished the Jews from Rome (Acts 18:1-2).
5. Nero -A.D. 54-68 (Caesar believed to have had Peter and Paul killed (2 Timothy 4:6-8; 2 Peter 1:13-14).
6. Galba-A.D. 68-69
7. Otho- A.D.69
8. Vitellius-A.D. 69
9. Vespasian -A.D. 69-79 (General charged with the Jerusalem rebellion of the 60's but upon Nero's death went to Rome to become emperor and left the task to his son Titus).
10. Titus -A.D. 79-81 (Son of Vapasian and the General who defeated Jerusalem on 70 A.D. (Matthew 24:1-34; Luke 21:20).
11. Domitian -A.D. 81-96 (Caesar who persecuted the Christians which probably served as the background for the wiring of the Apocalypse (Revelation).

CHAPTER FIFTEEN

Prophecy of the Ruler/King

I. Tribe – Judah

A. Jacob prophesied about the descendants of his son Judah.

'The scepter shall not depart from Judah, Nor the ruler's staff from between his feet, Until Shiloh comes, And to him shall be the obedience of the people.' (Genesis 49:10). The scepter shall not depart from Judah, **Shiloh** = Messiah.

Example-of a Kings scepter is found in the book of (Esther 4:11; 5:2).

B. **House of David.** God promised David he would always have a descendant on the throne.

"When your days are complete and you lie down with your fathers, I will raise up your descendant after you, who will come forth from you, and I will establish his kingdom.

He shall build a house for My name, and I will establish the throne of his kingdom forever. (2 Samuel 7:12-13).

II. Nature of the King

   A. Supernatural Daniel 7:13-14.

      1. Son of man- Human

      2. Riding on the clouds of heaven (God's prerogative). (Psalm 104:1-3, Psalms 97:1-2, Isaiah 19:1, Revelation 1:7-8).

Psalm 104:1-3 *Bless the LORD, O my soul! O LORD my God, You are very great;*

You are clothed with splendor and majesty, ² Covering Yourself with light as with a cloak, Stretching out heaven like a tent curtain. ³ He lays the beams of His upper chambers in the waters; He makes the clouds His chariot; He walks upon the wings of the wind.

REVELATION 1:7 BEHOLD, HE IS COMING WITH THE CLOUDS, *and every eye will see Him, even those who pierced Him; and all the tribes of the earth will mourn over Him. So it is to be. Amen.*

   B. Jesus is the God/Man (Colossians 2:9).

      1. God in the beginning (John 1:1-3).

      2. He became a man (John 1:14).

      3. Uniquely qualified mediate between God and man (1Timothy 2:5).

III. Spiritual Kingdom

   A. Made without hands (Daniel 2:45).
   B. Will endure forever (Daniel 2:44).
   C. Jesus kingdom not of this world.

      1. His kingdom is spiritual (John 18:36).
      2. He is the King of the Kingdom (Hebrews1:7-8).

Hebrews 1:7:8 And of the angels He says, "WHO MAKES HIS ANGELS WINDS, AND HIS MINISTERS A FLAME OF FIRE." ⁸ But of the Son He says, "YOUR THRONE, O GOD, IS FOREVER AND EVER, AND THE RIGHTEOUS SCEPTER IS THE SCEPTER OF HIS KINGDOM.

IV. Time, place and events. His birth and life foretold to his mother in Luke 1:31-33 *And behold, you will conceive in your womb and bear a son, and you shall name Him Jesus. ³² "He will be great and will be called the Son of the Most High; and the Lord God will give Him the throne of His father David; ³³ and He will reign over the house of Jacob forever, and His kingdom will have no end."*.

   A. Born in Bethlehem (Micah 5:2- Luke 2:4-6).
      Micah 5:2 *But as for you, Bethlehem Ephrathah, Too little to be among the clans of Judah, From you One will go forth for Me to be ruler in Israel. His goings forth are from long ago, From the days of eternity."*

(Micah was contemporary with Isaiah who wrote in about 755BC).

B. Born of a Virgin (Isaiah 7:14, Matthew 1:22, 23). *"Therefore the Lord Himself will give you a sign: Behold, a virgin will be with child and bear a son, and she will call His name Immanuel.* Isaiah 7:14

C. There would be a mass murder of the Hebrew boys (Jeremiah 31:15, Mt 2:16-18). Thus says the LORD, *"A voice is heard in Ramah, Lamentation and bitter weeping. Rachel is weeping for her children; She refuses to be comforted for her children, Because they are no more."* (Jeremiah 31:15), (Jeremiah prophesied in the 7th century BC a hundred years after Isaiah).

D. He would flee to Egypt (Numbers 24:8-Matthew 2:14,15) (Out of Egypt I will call my son).

E. He would be betrayed for 30 pieces of silver in which a potter's field would be purchased (Zechariah 11:12,13- Matthew 27:3-10).

F. He would be pierced (Zechariah 12:10, John 19:34,37)

G. Not a bone of him would be broken (Exodus 12:46/ John 19:33,36).

Time and Place

Under Roman Empire in Jerusalem Daniel 2:44, Micah 1:4

Isaiah 2:2-3 *Now it will come about that In the last days The mountain of the house of the LORD Will be established as the chief of the mountains, And will be raised above the hills;*

And all the nations will stream to it. 3 And many peoples will come and say, "Come, let us go up to the mountain of the LORD, To the house of the God of Jacob; That He may teach us concerning His ways And that we may walk in His paths." For the law will go forth from Zion And the word of the LORD from Jerusalem.

Luke 24:46-47 *and He said to them, "Thus it is written, that the Christ would suffer and rise again from the dead the third day, [47] and that repentance for forgiveness of sins would be proclaimed in His name to all the nations, beginning from Jerusalem.*

V. **Kingdom Fulfilled in** the 1st century. Prophecies of the Kingdom coming during Jesus' time

    A. John the baptizer (John 3:1,2).

    B. Jesus Matthew (4:17).

    C. Apostles (Matthew 10:7).

    D. The seventy (Luke 10:9).

    E. Jesus predicts that it will come soon

F. Some would still be alive (Mt 16:28, Mark 9:1, Lk 9:27).
G. Jesus Promised to build it (Matthew 16:18,19) (future)
H. The Kingdom is here now (Colossians 1:13) (present).

VI. Different roles of the Ruler.

A. Priest/sacrifice.(Hebrews 9:12) *and not through the blood of goats and calves, but through His own blood, He entered the holy place once for all, having obtained eternal redemption.*

B. Prophet. (Deuteronomy 18:15-18) *I will raise up a prophet from among their countrymen like you, and I will put My words in his mouth, and he shall speak to them all that I command.* Jesus is that prophet *Acts 3:22)

C. Founder/Builder (Matthew 16:18,19).

D. Foundation (1 Corinthians 3:11, Acts 4:11, Ephesians 2:2).

VII. The king seated on his throne

(Ephesians 1:19-23) and what is the surpassing greatness of His power toward us who believe. *These are* in accordance with the working of the strength of His might which He brought about in Christ, when He raised Him from the dead and seated Him at His right hand in the heavenly *places*, far above **all rule** and **authority** and **power** and **dominion**, and **every name that is named**, not only in this age but also in the one to come. And He put all things in subjection under His feet, and gave Him as head over all things to the church, which is His body, the fullness of Him who fills all in all.

    A. Raised-aorist (past one time action)

    B. Seated at right hand (Position of authority)- aorist

    C. Jesus is above *every power* and *every name now and* for all time.

        1. Rule ἀρχή [*arche*]-

        2. *Authority*-ἐξουσία [*exousia*]

        3. *Power*-δύναμις [*dunamis*]

        4. *Dominion*-κυριότης [*kuriotes* /

        5. *Name*-ὄνομα [*onoma* /

        6. Every age αἰών [*aion* /

Are you a citizen of the Kingdom Ruled by Jesus, the church of Christ?

Here's how to become one.

    Faith – Romans 10:17; Hebrews 11:6

    Repent- 2 Corinthians 7:9,10

    Confess- Matthew 16:16 ; Romans10:9,10,

    Baptism- Romans 6:3,4, Mt 28:19,20, Mark 16:15-16, 1 Peter 3:21

God bless you do it today.

BIBLIOGRAPHY

Flatt Bill. Personal Counseling a guide for Christian counselors and help for individuals working through personal and family problems toward positive solutions. Memphis: Flatt Publications, 1991.

http://www.americanaidfoundation.org/homeless%20comfort%20&%20care/Homeless%20Comfort%20&%20Care.html

https://afsp.org/about-suicide/suicide-statististics

https://www.biblegateway.com/passage/?search=1+tim+1&version=KJV

https://www.biblegateway.com/versions/New-American-Standard-Bible-NASB/

https://www.cdc.gov/nchs/fastats/adolescent-health.htm#

https://www.huduser.gov/publications/pdf/home_tech/tchap-13.

HTTPS://ENDHOMELESSNESS.ORG/HOMELESSNESS-IN-AMERICA/WHO EXPERIENCES-HOMELESSNESS/CHILDREN-AND-FAMILIES/

https://en.oxforddictionaries.com/

https://en.wikipedia.org/wiki/2012_Aurora_shooting

https://www.huduser.gov/publications/pdf/home_tech/tchap-13.pdf

http://live.denverpost.com/Event/Aurora_Theater_Shooting_July_20_2012?Page=0

http://www.nationalhomeless.org/factsheets/families.html

https://www.olympic.org/taekwondo

Kim Shik Dae (and others), Tae Kwon Do Forms Complete & Official Forms. The World Tae Kwon Do Federation. International Council on Martial Arts. Seoul, Republic Of Korea: 1988.

New American Standard Bible. The Lockman Foundation, 1995 update.

Sellers S. Crane, Jr. Truth For Today Commentary, AN EXEGESIS AND APPLICATION OF THE HOLY SPRIPTURES. Matthew 14-28. Benton. Resource Publications. 2011

Theological Dictionary of The New Testament Volume 1, Page 530

Edward Kruk, Ph.D., "The Vital Importance of Paternal Presence in Children's Lives." May 23, 2012.
http://www.psychologytoday.com/blog/co-parenting-after-divorce/201205/ father-absence-father-deficit-father-hunger

U.S. Census Bureau, Children's Living Arrangements and Characteristics: March 2011, Table C8. Washington D.C.: 2011

U.S. Department of Health and Human Services; ASEP Issue Brief: Information on Poverty and Income Statistics. September 12, 2012

www.ingramcontent.com/pod-product-compliance
Lightning Source LLC
LaVergne TN
LVHW051600080426
835510LV00020B/3064